D0613490

Book of beginning quintets
With exercises and techniques

By WALTER H. BARNES

Arranged for:
1st (B♭) Trumpet
→ 2nd (B♭) Trumpet
Horn in F
Trombone
Tuba
Conductor

THE CANADIAN BRASS EDUCATIONAL SERIES

DISTRIBUTED BY

HAL•LEONARD®
CORPORATION

7777 W. BLUEMOUND RD. P.O. BOX 13819 MILWAUKEE, WI 53213

Contents

E Easy   M Medium   D Difficult

A 'note' to you

Welcome to the ADVENTURE of Brass Ensembles! Now that you have learned the basic technique of playing, we want to introduce you to fine music in Quintet form. Here's where the fun really begins!

We have chosen simple but interesting tunes for you. Some are from the world of choral music which means that the phrases are just right for proper breathing, and the range is within one octave. Others are easy adaptations from well-known instrumental works by famous composers — songs that you and your audience will recognize. All selections are set in one of three beginning scales that you have probably already studied; almost all pieces are in   or   . (We have two pieces in 6 as a good learning experience.) All parts: — trumpets, french horn, trombone, tuba — are treated equally for equal development. Nowhere will you find the french horn and tuba relegated to the base job of Oom-Pah. The second trumpet has as much melody as the first. Many times the french horn and trombone are featured. And every selection relies on the tuba as the foundation, the support, the heart of the quintet.

Quintet means five. Five parts, not necessarily five players. We strongly suggest that you can use as many players per part as you have available. Involve all of your students and friends. Ensemble playing is more than good musical fun; it is a social interaction where each person or part stands equally and is necessary to the whole.

The key to this book and part of our own unique approach is found in the exercises set for each selection. We know that you will find them a real help in learning the piece. Use them carefully and repeatedly as you work towards the performance of the music. Listen to our cassette tape of this book. Try for the same Tone, Tuning, and Balance. Strive for the same smoothness and flow, and work towards the dynamics that we have given you.

When you have reached the plateau of #12, it's time to order

CANADIAN BRASS BOOK of EASY QUINTETS

and carry on in the finest form of musical experience: Ensemble Performance.

Have fun!

Canadian Brass

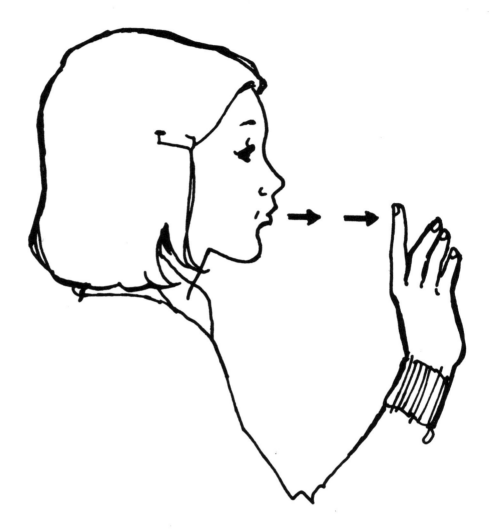

BREATHE IN
OPEN YOUR MOUTH CAVITY AND THROAT LIKE A YAWN!
BLOW AN AIR COLUMN TO YOUR FINGER
BREATHE IN — FEEL YOURSELF FILLING OUT
BLOW AN AIR COLUMN — 4 COUNTS
BREATHE IN — AIR DOWN
BLOW AN AIR COLUMN — 6 COUNTS
BREATHE IN — EXPAND LOW WITH AIR
BLOW AN AIR COLUMN — 8 COUNTS
BREATHE IN — FEEL AIR TO YOUR LOWER BACK
"BUZZ" A NOTE IN YOUR MOUTHPIECE — SEE NEXT PICTURE
AND INSTRUCTIONS

Warm-up

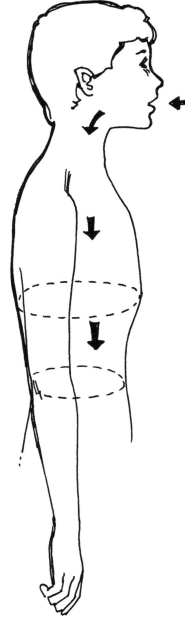

HOW DO WE START?

Just as a runner or swimmer stretches his muscles before he goes 'full out' in a race,

Just as we warm up our car before we put it into drive and move,

Just as we feel the water temperature before we jump into the pool,

We must prepare ourselves before we play.

The last thing we need is our instrument.

The first thing we need is air — deep breathing (Look at the picture)
body erect
ribs expanding
diaphragm expanding

Then, to our mouthpiece. (Look at the picture)
— find a comfortable middle range sound
— Buzz 4 beats, breathe 4 beats
— Buzz 6 beats, breathe 2 beats
— Make like a fire siren, up and down, up and down.
— Buzz your scale up and down
— Buzz tonguings, taking the rhythm of your piece
— Check the position of your mouthpiece in a mirror — keep centred.
— Buzz the piece you are about to work on

Now, we take out our instrument, and repeat the above steps, using the mouthpiece in the instrument, and playing the parts.

Make this pattern a regular part of your daily practice. We do.

6

HERE IS A GAME FOR YOU!
THERE ARE 18 ITALIAN MUSICAL TERMS.
LOOK EACH ONE UP IN YOUR MUSIC DICTIONARY TO FIND THE
ENGLISH MEANING.
THE NUMBER IN BRACKETS AFTER THE ITALIAN WORD TELLS
YOU THE NUMBER OF LETTERS IN THE ENGLISH WORD.
NOW, FIND THE ENGLISH WORD SOMEWHERE IN THE MAZE OF
LETTERS: VERTICAL
          HORIZONTAL
        OR DIAGONAL

Have fun!

S	F	R	E	Z	X	A	S	A	E	S	T	I	B	R	E	T	P	S	P
P	B	A	T	O	G	O	P	R	E	J	V	L	P	A	T	E	A	A	S
I	X	R	S	O	F	S	V	E	R	Y	L	O	U	D	O	R	U	S	I
V	O	W	A	T	B	T	I	W	P	O	E	Q	G	U	I	S	O	B	L
E	D	I	E	X	E	I	W	O	S	P	H	T	O	O	M	S	P	H	U
R	N	R	O	B	Y	R	D	L	M	I	F	B	W	L	R	G	B	B	S
O	E	O	O	L	B	G	J	S	O	O	T	M	M	M	A	R	L	I	A
R	J	L	W	T	A	I	R	O	S	F	J	U	T	U	T	O	T	C	A
A	B	O	S	D	Q	H	A	M	W	I	R	S	A	I	U	Q	I	O	F
T	L	O	S	R	E	S	U	A	P	T	O	B	J	D	L	S	A	W	P
S	F	I	F	U	G	I	M	Q	S	I	T	I	E	E	V	J	H	R	R
S	M	O	P	M	D	U	J	N	U	E	T	R	A	M	P	P	I	O	O
O	J	I	S	E	T	D	I	L	T	I	N	L	P	T	V	S	F	J	M
T	L	O	M	Y	X	S	E	L	F	P	C	R	X	U	G	T	P	A	Z
E	L	H	A	G	R	T	P	N	O	Q	A	K	A	P	I	F	L	D	Q
R	G	I	L	A	S	E	T	L	L	U	F	T	L	B	L	O	U	D	I
M	E	F	L	O	U	S	V	A	M	Y	B	F	A	Y	R	S	T	E	M

SUBITO (8)
LEGATO (6)
PP (4) (4)
FERMATA (5)
F (4)
ALLEGRO (7)
TUTTI (4)
MP (6) (4)
LENTO (6)

RITARD (6)
P (4)
CRESCENDO (6)
ACCELERANDO (6)
STACCATO (5)
FF (4) (4)
FINE (3)
MF (6) (4)
DIMINUENDO (6)

Scales for Trumpet

Music from the Royal Fireworks

HANDEL

In 1748, the treaty of *Aix-la-Chapelle* was signed to create peace in Europe, especially between England, Holland, Austria, and their opponents France, Spain and Prussia. In 1749, Handel was commissioned to compose the *Royal Fireworks* to celebrate (with real fireworks!) the first anniversary of the Treaty. This theme is the final Menuet of the Suite.

Scale of: G (The 2 Octave scale is shown for reference to all notes.)

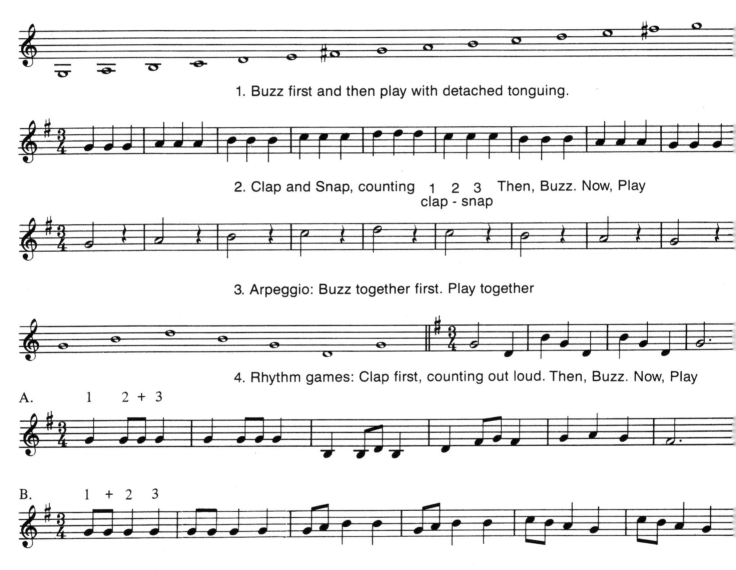

1. Buzz first and then play with detached tonguing.

2. Clap and Snap, counting   1   2   3   Then, Buzz. Now, Play
   clap - snap

3. Arpeggio: Buzz together first. Play together

4. Rhythm games: Clap first, counting out loud. Then, Buzz. Now, Play

A.   1   2 + 3

B.   1 + 2   3

5. This is your first note. It will be a chord. Tune your note to the Tuba. Play first to get pitch, then Buzz IN TUNE. LISTEN! Now, Play IN TUNE.

1. Music from the Royal Fireworks

Handel
(1685–1759)

Ode to Joy

BEETHOVEN

One of the world's great melodies, this theme was composed by Beethoven for the Finale of his Ninth Symphony. Note the simplicity of it; it is a string of sounds, stepping rather than leaping, rising and falling, supported by simple but rich harmony.

Scale of: F

The flattened fourth note makes a half-tone between the third and fourth. As well, there is always a half-tone between the seventh and eighth note.

Find the first note using your instrument. Then Buzz the exercise, working on smooth tonguing (the Tip of the Tongue) and Tuning with each other. Now, play on your instrument.

This is your first note. Play it on your instrument.

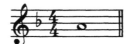

Now, sing it, tuning to the rest of the group.

Sing the exercise, breathing at the double bars. TUNE the Harmony.

Now, Buzz the line, again tuning carefully.
Now, play it, listening and tuning the chords.

Do the same steps to the line below

You will notice a double bar at the end of bar 16. Double bars are used to show the end of one section and the beginning of another, just like paragraphs are used in stories.

2. Ode to Joy

Beethoven
(1770–1827)

Sanctus — from the German Mass

SCHUBERT

Schubert was one of the greatest melody writers. In this very simple work for choir, he gives every part a melodic line. Since the Sanctus is from Choral Literature, you will find that the breath marks give you the phrasing.

Scale of: F

Now, play the scale in the rhythm below.

This is the first note of your scale in 4/4 time

If you want a four beat note in 3/4 time, you write it like this. This is a tie.

Play your first note.

Now, sing it.
Sing the line below, then buzz it, then play it, TUNING CAREFULLY. Listen all around you, especially to the Tuba.

Follow the same steps with this line. The middle chord is different.

Now, try this line — singing first, then buzzing, then playing.

Hint: When performing the Sanctus, watch the change of harmony in bar 25-6, and the different rhythm in bar 27 for 2 parts.

After you have worked on Sanctus a few times, try to sing the entire piece in Harmony. Do not worry if your voice cannot sing in the instrumental range. BREATHE EXACTLY TOGETHER.

3. Sanctus

Schubert
(1797-1828)

14

Saint Anthony

HAYDN

Haydn wrote this simple Chorale originally for Woodwinds. Brahms used it for his great Variations on a Theme of Haydn. We have arranged it as a Brass Quintet featuring the French Horn and the Trombone, while the Tuba, as ever, anchors the harmonies.

Scale of C

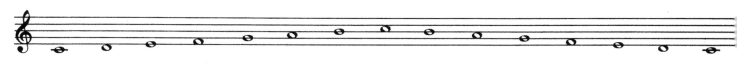

Now buzz the scale in the pattern below, taking care that the Tip of the Tongue is up behind the front teeth on the gum. Do this as smoothly as you possibly can. Now, play the scale in the pattern — up and down — smoothly and with a nice crescendo up.

There is only one Rhythmic trick-spot in the Chorale: Bar 5. Count to four; clap your rhythm; buzz your part; play your part. The Tuba has one rhythm, the French Horn and Trombone join in another, and the two Trumpets have a pick-up.

Bar ⑤ 1 2 3 + 4 + ⑥ 1 2 3 4

Hint: Take note of the 'staggered' breathing that we have used in places. Follow your markings exactly, and the total effect will be much smoother.

Question: Have you ever seen a piece with five-bar phrases before? We have written the Chorale in four. When you have learned the piece, think of two beats per measure $\frac{2}{2}$ rather than $\frac{4}{4}$

4. Saint Anthony

Haydn
(1732-1809)

Amazing Grace

EARLY AMERICAN

Originally, the tune of this Hymn was a tavern song. John Newton, a slave-trader for almost 20 years of his life, was converted and became a Minister of the Gospel in Liverpool! He wrote the words that have made this melody famous, and which brought it from the beer halls to the gospel halls.

Scale of: G (written for playing range)

Buzz the scale in tune to the pattern below. Now, play it smoothly. Follow the breathing exactly, both times.

Do the same for the three exercises below

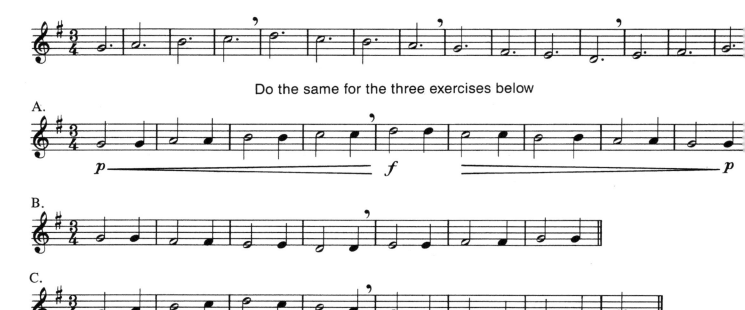

This rhythmic fragment is bar 9 to 12. The problem is to get a clean release on the quarter rest, and to enter together on the next note. Buzz first, then play; *stop* the air — DO NOT CUT IT OFF WITH THE TONGUE.

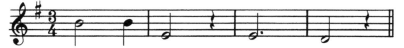

Now, indulge the first Trumpet part. This time, there is an extra note as a pick-up during the quarter rests. Buzz and play.

This is your last note of the piece. Choose a leader if your teacher is not present, and have him or her give a *slight* nod for the cut off. Come off together without using the tongue. The 'eyebrow' is a FERMATA. It means to hold the note until satisfied.

5. Amazing Grace

Early American

Westminster Abbey

PURCELL

Westminster Abbey is an ancient church in London, England. Most of the Kings and Queens have been crowned in that magnificent building which is just across the road from the Parliament Buildings. Henry Purcell was Organist at Westminster in 1679. He is buried in a vault at the foot of the Great Organ.

In order to perform this piece in its true style, visualize a great cathedral with its echoes and space.

Scale of: G

Arpeggio: Find your first note on your instrument; Buzz, then Play.

Lipping Exercise: Find your note, Buzz, Play, Buzz, Play, Buzz, Play.

There are two Rhythmic difficulties:

Bar 5 — 8. Find your note; Count 1 — 2 — 3 — ; Count and Clap; Buzz the Rhythm; Play the exercise.

Now, Buzz, then Play these notes in the same Rhythm.

Bar 13 — 16. Follow the same steps as above.

Now, Buzz, then Play these notes in that Rhythm.

6. Westminster Abbey

Purcell
(1658-1695)

Steal Away

SPIRITUAL

Spirituals are true forms of folk music: unknown composer or group created, reflecting the thoughts and needs of the community. The American Black in slavery sang about freedom after death. A strong religious conviction in the text was supported by simple harmony choruses and unison verses. 'Steal Away' is a fine example of this form, and of the power and glory found in Spirituals.

"Steal away to Jesus; I ain't got long to stay here. My Lord, He calls me; the Trumpet sounds within my soul."

Scale of: F

Here is the scale in an unusual pattern. Take care to make the second note of each bar three full beats. Breathe together and re-enter together. Buzz the scale up *and down*; now, Play up and down.

In this pattern, the trick is to keep the air column unbroken with that little nasty eighth note. Barely touch it. Buzz, then Play.

Unison: Everyone playing the same note (here, in Octaves).
We have isolated one short phrase for you.
Find your first note; then Buzz it together, *tuning* to each other.

THIS IS DIFFICULT!

Now, Play the phrase, eliminating all the wavers between parts.

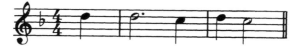

Try it in combinations: All trumpets
                           trumpets and tuba
                           trombone and tuba
                           french horn and tuba
                           your choice of combination
The rest of the group listen and criticize. Eliminate wavers! Good Luck!

7. Steal Away

Spiritual

Echo Carol

CHRISTMAS

Imagine two groups of people singing the same song; one group is around you, and one group is far away. The echo effect is created by the dynamic changes. If your ensemble has two or more people per part, try dividing into two halves, with the first group playing the first four bars, the second group playing the echo: — bar 5 — 8. Follow this pattern to the end.

Scale of: C

Pattern: Breathe only where marked — NOT after the dotted half note,

Dynamics: Different volumes without altering pitch or tone.
f is forte which is *loud*; p is piano which is *soft*.
Find your note. Now,
Buzz loudly, tuning;
Buzz softly, tuning, keeping air and throat open.
Don't pinch the air.
Play loudly, tuning;
Play softly, tuning and keeping the same bright tone.
(Hard, isn't it?)

Now, repeat the same exercises for these two notes.
Repeat the entire process over and over, listening carefully to you and the entire group. Sometimes, have one member of your group listen and report.

Here is the first phrase, isolated for you. Follow the instructions above.

The only other problem you will have is tuning this phrase, going from Unison to a Major chord to a Minor chord. Buzz. then Play very slowly, listening very carefully. Try singing your parts.

8. Echo Carol

À la Claire Fontaine

FRENCH

Though French in origin, this song was brought to Canada in 1605 by Champlain's men. It became a symbol to the French Canadian who vowed never to forget his motherland. The simple but haunting melody is perfect for the brass player to develop a singing and flowing line. Not always are we to be loud and forceful!

Scale of: G

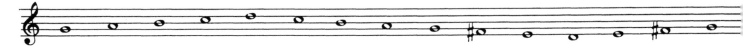

Pattern: Lean on the half note slightly, while easing back on the two quarter notes. Use a very gentle tonguing.
"Tip of the Tongue" (say that 10 times with the *tip* of the tongue just touching the gum above the front teeth).

Balance: We have isolated a phrase for you.

Step 1
2nd Trumpet, French Horn, Trombone, Tuba
Play the phrase so smoothly. Now, play it softer.
Each part has a melody of its own. Make it melodious.

Step 2
Add the 1st Trumpet, with the other four parts supporting, but not covering. The 1st Trumpet should not play louder; the other four should play softer.

Step 3
Repeat this phrase, Buzzing, Singing, Buzzing and Playing, until you have found the magical flow and harmonic tuning that you hear on the tape.

Note: At the end of bar 57 is a ∥ Grand Pause. Come right off, breathe together, and enter together.

9. À la Claire Fontaine

French

Processional

GERMAN

This is a fine rhythmic marching tune. We have chosen it specifically for its scale passages, and as an excellent exercise for Unison to Harmony playing. Listen to our recording of the Toccata in D Minor. Following a Unison opening, we build a complex harmonic chord. Listening and Tuning is the key to success for both you and for us.

Scale of: C

This piece is in $\frac{6}{4}$. There are: six beats in one bar
one quarter note gets one beat

Each of the following bars gets six beats. Play the scale in each pattern.

Note that from bar 1 — 16, each phrase is presented once and repeated once. We have isolated the first phrase and removed the bar lines to show you. Now, you isolate the next five phrases.

From Unison to Harmony: Use each exercise, tuning the first note harmonizing the second note slowly and carefully

The final two bars has a counting problem. Bar 31 is shown below:

1st Trumpet	2nd Trumpet	French Horn	Trombone	Tuba
6	2:4	4:2	2:4	2:4

Bar 31

10. Processional

German

Crimond

SCOTTISH

From the great wealth of Scotland's psalm tunes, we have selected our favourite, Crimond. The tune is made up of 2 *seven* bar phrases. We feature the Trumpets in verse one, while the other instruments support; in verse two, the French Horn and Trombone have the melody. Verse three is almost the same as verse one. Do your best, if you are in a supporting role, to help the solo. Listen constantly for tuning and balance. Your audience will better appreciate your performance.

Scale of: G

Pattern:

Rhythm: Using the pattern below: Clap the rhythm
find your note and Buzz the rhythm
Play the rhythm

Now, Trumpets, French Horn and Trombone go to the notes below, while the Tuba Claps the pattern above
Buzzes the pattern above
Plays the pattern above

Lipping Exercise: (to help with the Tpts entry at bar 1, and the F.H. and Tbne entry at bar 15).

Hint: An accidental in a bar lasts for the entire bar.
It is cancelled by the bar line (or another accidental)
Trumpets: check bar 6; French Horn and Trombone: check bar 20.

11. Crimond

Scottish

Chorale

BACH

We have chosen the famous Chorale that Bach chose to elaborate for his magnificent Chorale Prelude: Jesu, Joy of Man's Desiring. This is a more difficult piece than any preceding. The breathing must be as marked, which forces a rather quick tempo. The dynamics must be as marked, which puts an even harder demand on the performer. (When you have completed this selection, order our Book of Easy Quintets; you'll be ready for some selections at that plateau.)

Scale of: G

Breathing: Find your note on your instrument.
Play the exercise below, with the entire group breathing together on each rest.

Now, follow the same procedure with this exercise. The two dots before the double bar means to repeat the line.

Try this line. Listen to the rest of your group breathe. Re-enter together.

Ornaments: Ornaments are a form of decoration, like icing on the cake. They are not essential to this Chorale. For this piece, as for all pieces ever, learn the music before you attempt the ornaments.

Ornament #1 is for bar 7, 15, 31 in the First Trumpet,
bar 39, 47, 63 in the F.H. and Tbne.
Ornament #2 is for bar 19 in the First Trumpet, and
bar 51 in the F.H. and Tbne,
Ornament #3 is for bar 23 in the First Trumpet, and
bar 55 in the F.H. and Tbne.

12. Chorale

Bach
(1685-1750)

In a singing style; ♩=90

32

Tudor Motet

TYE

From the choral literature of 16th C. England, we have chosen this simple motet. The range for all instruments is easy; most notes go by step rather than by a difficult leap. Since the music was written for singing, the phrases are short and provide logical breathing spaces. But, since the music is polyphonic (everyone has an equal melody) rather than homophonic (chordal), the performance of this piece will provide your group with a challenge. We have graphed the music for you. Follow your own part; colour your own line. Notice that your phrases have the same shape as other parts but are played at different times. Try to imitate the other parts in the style of playing. You will find other examples and much more detail of this polyphonic writing in our *Easy Book of Quintets*.

Have fun!

Scale of: F

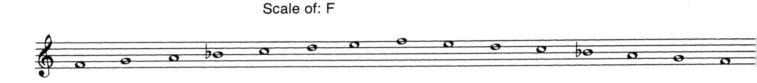

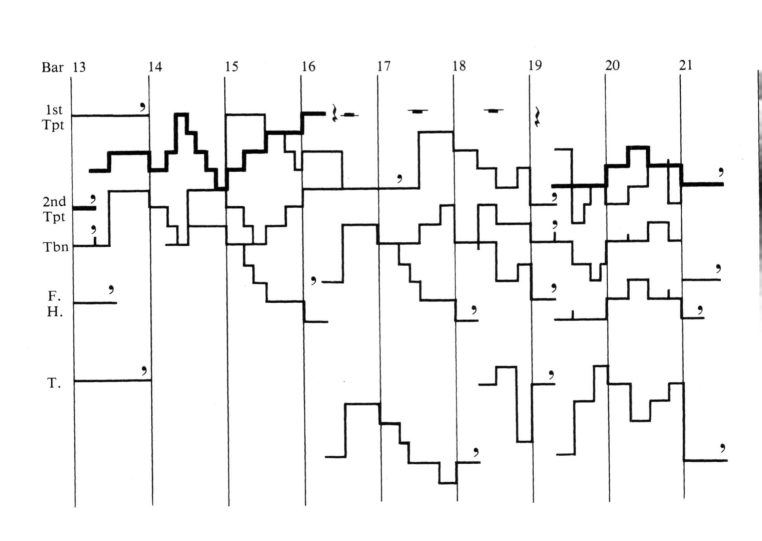

13. Tudor Motet

Tye
(1497-1572)

Kelligrew's Soirée
(A Newfoundland Jig)

CANADIAN

Here, we have a very popular folk song of Newfoundland, with a characteristically Irish flavour. The 2:1 ratio of the rhythm must predominate at all times. The music must proceed with a bounce and flair that one would find at a Saturday night dance in a small fishing village on the rough wild shores of Newfoundland.

Scale of: G

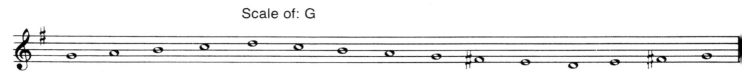

Rhythm: $\frac{6}{8}$ time: six beats in a bar, with an eighth note getting 1 beat.

When you have learned this piece, count 2 beats

Ratio: 2: 1 in a bar: 1 - - 2 - - | 1 - - 2 - - |

Say together: *Quar-ter eighth Quar-ter eighth*

1	2	1	1	2	1
1	2	3	4	5	6

Exercises: Rhythmic Patterns: Clap; Buzz; Play repeatedly on the first note; Play to the Scale pattern.

14. Kelligrew's Soirée
(A Newfoundland Jig)

Canadian

Fanfare for a Maple Leaf
(A Canadian Brass Buzz)

CANADIAN

This Fanfare was written especially for You! Rhythmically, it looks difficult, but if you follow the instructions below, it is very easy.

∧ is the sign for a very strong *Accent*. This is accomplished with an intensity of air and the tongue forming a "te" rather than a "ta" (in other words, more pointed). Whenever you have the *Accent*, you must project your sound to the fore of the group. Within the Fanfare, there is a hidden melody which will be brought out if the *Accents* are followed.

The Fanfare should be played strongly to the end. Bar 21 shows a 'p' for soft. This is a *volume* marking; the effect should be a quiet intensity, with the same strength as the preceding 20 bars, which are marked 'f' for loud.

Instructions

1. Clap Rhythm
2. Play first note for pitch
3. Buzz first note
4. Buzz the rhythm of the entire piece on that one note
5. Buzz the rhythm, this time sounding the notes as written
6. Play the rhythm on your first note
7. Play the Fanfare as written, on your instrument
8. Rehearse, making the eighth notes short and clean, and putting more weight on all the whole notes
9. Strive for a brightness of tone, a clean attack, and precise cut-offs.

15. Fanfare for a Maple Leaf

(A Canadian Brass 'Buzz')

Canadian

Battle Hymn of the Republic

AMERICAN

The Battle Hymn is the best-known of all American songs. It is sung and played in schools, churches, at campfires and sing-songs. It is a true part of the American heritage. It is known throughout the world as a hymn, a Civil War song and a march tune. Here, it is set for Brass Quintet.

The arrangement starts as it finishes: quietly, distantly and dramatically. The Trombone carries the melody, with the French Horn on a counter-melody. Trumpets: keep your mini-fanfares short and clean. Watch the change of key at bar 32 — 40. Have fun!

Scale of: C

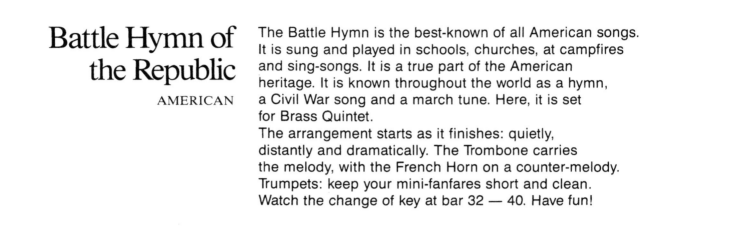

Math Lesson: to accomplish the correct playing of a ♩.♪ for Battle Hymn.

```
0   0   0  :  0
1   2   3  :  1
```

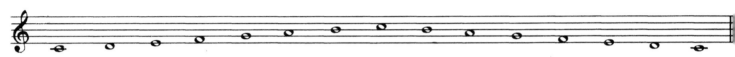

All these are three to one ratio. Therefore, make sure your sound is a three: one ratio. Count and clap on 1 and 4

1 2 3 4 1 2 3 4 1 2 3 4 1 2 3 4 1 2 3 4 1 2 3 4 1 2 3 4 1 2 3 4

Scale Patterns:

A.

B.

16. Battle Hymn of the Republic

American

A 'note' on performance

It's been a real joy, working through this book with you. We've had a chance to give you many of our ideas; we've shared some of our favourite pieces with you. It's been a personal thing from your teacher and from us — to you.

Now, it's your turn to share music with others. Your first audience will probably include family members who have heard you practice all the pieces, but have no concept of the total sound of all five parts. Here are some ideas to help you plan your programme.

Don't choose to play a piece that you cannot guarantee — under the stress of a public concert — success. Choose pieces from the Book that your group can perform well, even though you might be nervous.

Choose a variety of pieces thinking of tempos, dynamics, keys, and who has the melody. You might start off with the Fanfare, and end with your favourite selection. Use a contrasting piece in the middle.

Remember that your concert starts from the moment that you walk on stage until you are off. Be careful that nothing you do will detract from the music.

Your excitement for the music that you are playing will infect the audience and bring them great pleasure.

Have Fun!
The Canadian Brass

Next Step: *Canadian Brass Book of Easy Quintets*